VIGILANCE IS NO ORCHARD

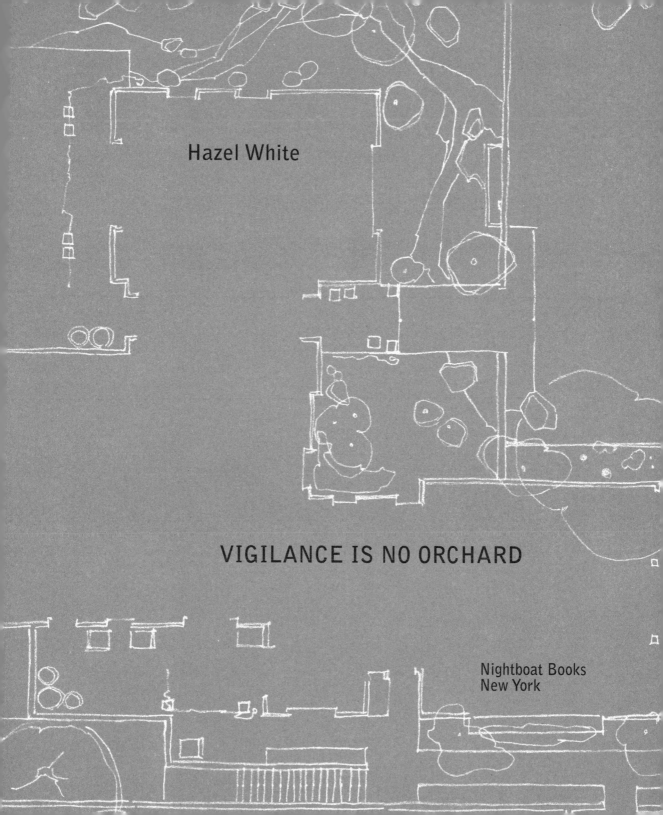

Hazel White

VIGILANCE IS NO ORCHARD

Nightboat Books
New York

ISBN 978-1-937658-82-3

Design and typesetting by Margaret Tedesco
Text set in Bell Gothic and Berling
Cover and interior photographs: Marion Brenner
Interior art: Landscape plans of Carol Valentine project,
Montecito, California, hand-drawn in 1981 by Isabelle Greene *C*
Courtesy of the artists

Cataloging-in-publication data is available
from the Library of Congress

Distributed by University Press of New England
One Court Street
Lebanon, NH 03766
www.upne.com

Nightboat Books
New York
www.nightboat.org

for Isabelle

CONTENTS

You only look at Flowers *quite gently. It's like an idea that emerges out of the background, appears and then turns pale again. In turn this means a security, a conviviality, a coziness, that are not right, that you can't really touch.*
—Luc Tuymans

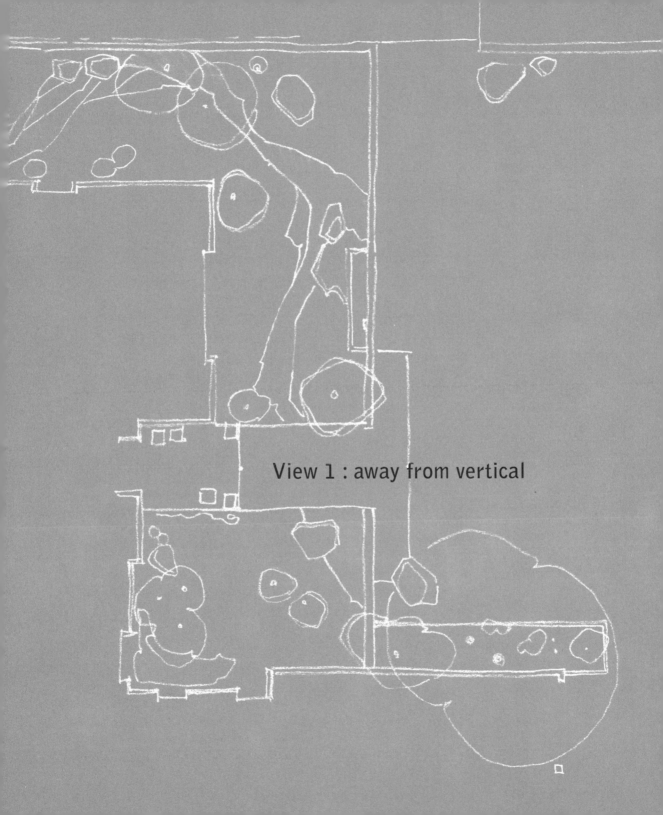

View 1 : away from vertical

Finding a photograph of the Valentine garden, my gaze locked. Then my elbow
dropped. I was holding something.

Writing had become turgid, ordinant; whereas this garden—with yarrow flowers
and lilies, both ribbed—unfolded shockingly flat.

A view encourages distribution, so I set out to advance beyond habit,

to the entrance, which landscape architect Isabelle Greene shaped low and open
to draw a visitor forward.

Seventeen years pass, and I'm looking back to tell the Valentine story from all points of contact:

Terraces that step down gently were a clue that Greene intended a seamless departure. My feet anchored in groundcover, my head could ride the lines there, on air's back.

Also, the pond, where to hang under the reeds on the slate over the water is gulping shelter and view at once, and I plunged into reflection and lugged the light in the sky back to the firm rock.

I bowed low to Greene's motion. Accepted the blow of it—I must know the how of its thinnest leaf on its strongest breeze, be sure, as my back was bending in astonishment.

I would trespass. Attention iterating, amplifying, manic, exactly how I had dreamt it.

Let me turn up the volume: My acquaintance with the image did not begin dimly. I lost my brisket, I mean basket.

Weight rolled off the page; risk bought it. Synthesis of direction and what to do. Then was no time for figuring, fingering, if this hillside might stall all navigation.

"What was missing was a strong vertical. The yuccas and agaves will bloom and there will be something momentarily tall. But it's not nearly enough. I needed something at eye level that starts down there and comes up to you" (Greene).

In awe of her, shyly I proposed a half lie, and she declined it.

Again, for three years, until my devotion steered language to volume, line, thrill, tapped a recalcitrant orientation and

she spilled a fierce polyandrous vocabulary of making,
propagative sinew of a silence that had sloughed off safety.

We touched it. We clinched it.

"I don't like walls. I don't like separation."

Beauty is not shelter, it necessitates a forward momentum,
so my desire, though the phrasing small and never named as envy: I would/I
wished/I would/write about her.

I came out with it.

Beginning over, in Greene's miniature agriculture. Wide-eyed aerial aspect into fields of nurture. Urgently, I went.

The yellow-blue motility of canyon light and ocean air an equivalency of in and out of thought, a traveling part of this.

Arrival. Fat odor of rising summer. Dry sage—and fog pulling off Santa Barbara Bay.

I'll revisit each preposition: The bridge off the lane sharpens the body to over (the creek), and then the crunch of gravel in the entrance court, and my wheels rolling on to. Into the frame and eyeing the vine on the wall ranging up and over and along, not leaving any part of itself behind.

I'll step out of before, outside the garden, where litter of the gulley, bucket/crease of leaves, galore of boulders, no typical size, bake.

White walls part the garden from the hillside oaks. "That's hard on me."

To make a garden or a text show up—one needs the connections to be manifold. "But I hate geometry." Instead, she trusts loose horizontals, extensions wide and visceral:

Because real work is hospitality, a cloud dispersing to what's beneath, sky opens to surround it.

Besides, diagonally, the oak branches lean toward/over the walls, go reflexively to surplus, and blood beats in greeting—

Her constructions cross the hill against the wind and sun, pull the space taut to demonstrate the filigree of survival.

Tangles eased out in coincidences and moving things about:

      no focal point, rather

      a bauhinia tree with horizontal branches, and just below it to one side, a bauhinia shrub, espaliered, so "white-flowering, naturally floaty layers reflect the lines of the white stucco walls"—as in tango with, kiss back, one.

I chose immersion.

When space conjoins like that, as in the image in the magazine—vault between spine stem and ribs broad and green, and the air—

Wait for me.

This wants not to be a strong narrative; the take-away should be an interior motion, jaw and sacrum, say, letting go together, to release the neck and then the head flies up.

When the landscape architect first crossed the garden threshold, she found a place to pee.

View 2 : the way about

A project arrives as space.

Figure what is given:

mountain backdrop
alluvial fan to the sea
"at the edge inventing"

"Try dill—or Queen Anne's lace—threaded through a cedrela grove, or Gold Plate
achillea (yarrow) threaded through plant stakes."

Try talkback. Try leapfrogging bewilderment with a
readiness to act.

Make a rustle.

Not a metaphysical hum
from over the horizon but something presently large in the bush
in the hand.

Currency strums through the sternum sideways along the shoulder bones to the back, which is a text, not a mass, but movement, each rib loose, the way life is. Fly it?

I ride it. Sounds may rocket out of the mouth.

Not authority, an upright, fastigiate, which is rearguard, but a physical forward and away (do I mean a changing body schema, what's palpably overrunning bilateral symmetry?)—

Thank you for the Easter card, I tell her.

Anyway, it crosses into space never looking back, like a manuscript bearing the distractions of temper, even cheerfulness.

Seeks a workable shape, goes until it's there.

Grazing roughly the image of garden, for the salt of habitat: laurel, swans, and watercress—

to have an environment whole, brown, green and blue, round and deep, forest and fields engorged, not parceling or steering into writing:

land's edge zones   parked in one's interior territories,

hungrily making   rooms for them.

Enterprise getting off the ground and staunchly emerald,

yet the hillside at the Valentine garden is turning thrifty.

Beauty howling off the image,

creates a grave disorientation,
                    clumsy
          shift
in
                                                            pivot/
                                              into

thinning
bruising
          switch
-eroos.

"I collect quotes. I like talking through others."

"Here, from the letters of Sylvia Townsend Warner, 'if one wants to enjoy the possession of an oak tree, one must plant it in the village of nowhere in the province of nothingness.' "

Land outside the garden buttery and rugged, undirected, voluptuous, strict. I, in my soft container, tapping its lexicon of performance so engagement can be figured out.

Wanting to be animate/exchangeable. A body in 3D:

> girth of the pomegranate tree
> photosynthesis certain of itself
> "I told him not to claw at the rock face but to stick the blade
> straight down and push away huge chunks"

Then satisfaction with the surroundings grows physical as in bending in almost no wind.

A garden offers ready-made (primordial) satisfactions. Trust it.

Awareness of its forms alerts the body, so if I am quick
I can prod spatial pleasure for the texture of attention—

While the intellect is confounded, I tattle over the threshold as the eucalyptus beats
the house and sets off again sailing in air, or the vine grows springy and rapidly over
the wall toward the (built) spring that is a metaphor for a Sierra Nevada spring, the
situation
      —running ahead of myself,
           rolling off the tongue.

I'm free to speak loosely and a predator could easily be seen.

With curiosity as passkey, I'll know what's near.

Wait—

Working low to the earth—is Greene timid and showing no tail? A landscape architect in Napa runs soaring poplars in lines parallel to the house, and where the unashamed geometry meets the canyon at an insufficiently tall wall, the point of contact sparks as in a lightning field, as it should do! There, we are carried by repetition of line far from our self-righteousness, and at the end of what we know, Time Before whistles in from the outside. It othered me, gave me a big earache, threatened to take down my pants. I couldn't return a jangled cup to its smooth saucer. On top of it, the marsh outside the insufficiently tall wall was full of red-winged blackbirds shrieking delightedly.

I'll continue the argument later.

View 3 : what wants to occur

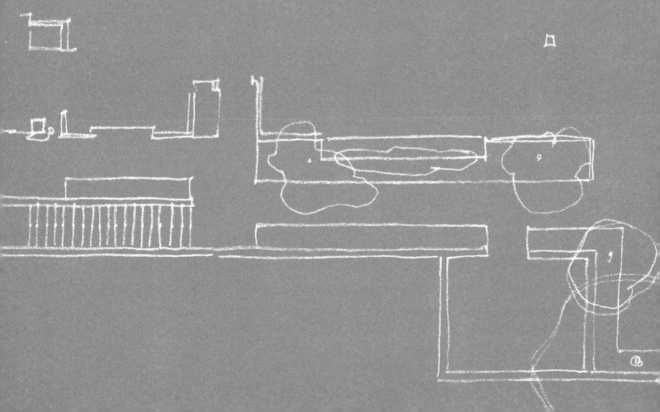

Cleverness doesn't cut it at the threshold from one experience to another. A bird flits from boulder to boulder—tries out a nook near the water, swoops right by here, as in a plot twist, or something sprouting in the heat of meeting, with no pause as being goes slickly through the slipknot into doing.

The breeze comes
up and down the ditch, to my wrist, whispers up my sleeve, grows less identical with
itself through the comfort of enclosure.

Write as a limb sways,

as the *Eucalyptus citriodora,* lankily over the roof, casts off nonchalantly,
many leaves or taking leave, intention lost. This all explorative along a midrib.

"Cow parsnips riffling among quaking aspens, horizontals floating through verticals."

Water to plants, intimate. Foliage solicitous, not apart.

Unearth what wants to occur in this space.

Put a stake in the ground.

Loot and hollow out.

Build a lodge braced against the shore, bower painted with the juice of berries, uproot stems and push them over and back over one another.

Make concretions, then glance away and quickly
back, to snatch the motion in stories that aren't so obvious—I'll holler until they
hold.

"When it arches up . . . , put a path right underneath."

Placing objects beside extensions, processing, repurposing, stamping.

Circulations: blood, irrigation, prospering.

Brazen goings-on.

Mutual life—and voyeuristic opportunity. In toto,

a wild empiricism racing to a jumping-off point:

Take this picture.

Sealing with mud, shaping momentum,
not simply draping with plants.

      Reset myself

plural,

again and again, greeting each vibrant word and dispersal,

shuttling between systems exceeding themselves, something I already know how to do,

      hump jumping onto it.

A field day, as wasps know, crawling split fruit.

Visiting the Valentine garden, I trespass and steal figs. Purple juice puts blood back in my enterprise. This isn't voice, but sinew in the summer heat, an open realm. Harvest uttering carnally.

I want to live in the green. And this wants out of me onto the page.

"Work larger,"
vow of felting syllables
becoming encounters—a series, far
out ahead of synthesis—strew
and align them.

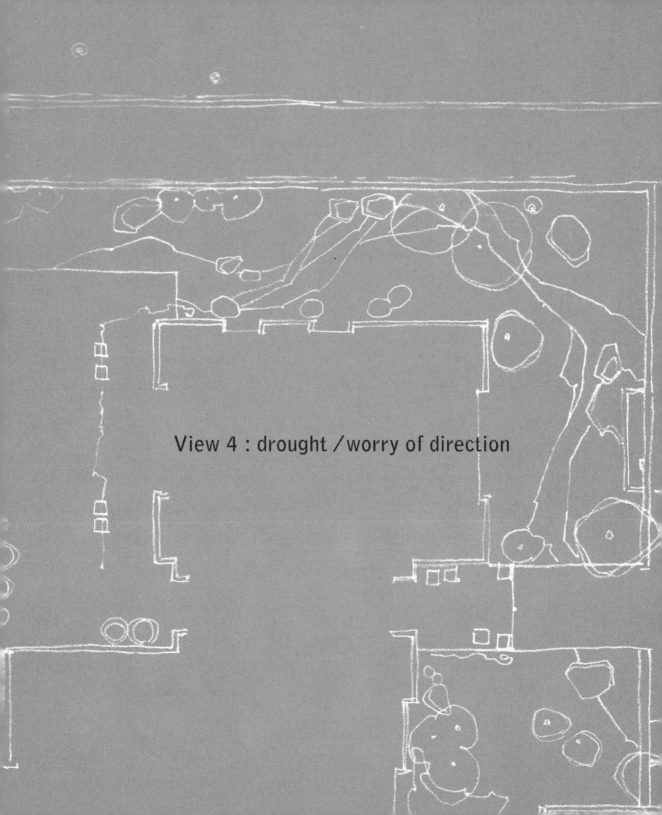

View 4 : drought / worry of direction

This anything but an easy architecture of yellow and blue in our lap. Vision retreating cavalierly. I wanted the journey to assure me, that in rereading this, I would find that I, like Greene, am planting a vine over the facts to welcome a visitor home today. But my hand goes vicariously, obsequiously, when text like land must be worked in the real. Her work gaining on space, yet I have been unable to press forward so inevitably. My motion has gone as stolons, making brief lines radially, when sustained axiality would be the way to make the project one. Wishing the distance were a single high dive, the tallest climb and

the drop the farthest words can go,
not a false investigation,
full weights.

By habit, I smooth my skirt. It takes courage to enter my geometry.

Stature, status, estate, inculcate, and institute:
whiteness and voice, massive ideograms.

Whereas what there is to see, I can look at:

to left and right, water seemingly rising, flows,
eye flows, picks up and off, concentrically, around
the weeping mayten
tree.
In raked gravel circles, the breeze
is a light express,
merry-

Once more the text and gravel go—
under my feet—the straight-to-the-door path

forgetting, become again a bridge—

"something at eye level that starts down there . . ."

carried on stepping-stones to the pond.

36

Pulled underwater by a fragmented narrative. Refracted. 4D. Sunk beneath the surface, chewing beneath the vine springing.

Such open-handed feeding—that's flirtatious landscape architecture.

"It's a dreaming thing. If a woman loves flowers, there'll be all kinds of perennials," repetition of like characteristics, a landscape pleasure.

Then relief from the personal smells good. Plot dissolves to tableau, simply for viewing, a gaze through glass toward no particular direction.

California sunlit land.

          My know-how,
           willow it.

             Crack

                    to make place
                  grow again.

The scope is not fixed—

I approached the garden with legs flowing away from chest, not speaking through this of something else. Land getting on with it, in production though not spruced or remembering and not meaning or diagnostic. But I am writing aesthetically, aphoristically, over pastel escarpments where light spreads uninterrupted, feeding birdlike, not speaking out loud. Now I must mash the remaining unspoken underripeness. What's my say-so? The work arcs and fails. Vision and knowing held apart. The garden itself no longer generating where this will go.

If there were a manner in which language might push out and touch us—"run through the body like the light before a storm,"

exactly what relief and spring look like.

"It's confirmed at the Lovelace tea house and down on everybody's calendars. Hooray, you'll be here, close, in town for a while."

"My shows at the Santa Barbara Museum of Art and the UCSB Museum were an immensely enlarging experience. There was ME! All my life, so hard to express something, ever since I was a baby, wanted to get something inside me out."

At the Lovelace garden, down San Ysidro Lane, a meadow under oaks lengthens toward moisture. Grasses tuft, throat clearing.

I arrived once, an architect come west on a wagon seat, planted my head in the hut, and ranged for information.

Now many years later, adept at losing shelter, knowing also what a view extracts from me, an evolutionary arrangement, I learn

this Lovelace tunnel of light and land slanting holds the mouth soft to allow an easy birthing.

"A feeling for the crease in an arroyo, down in it and way back up the other side."

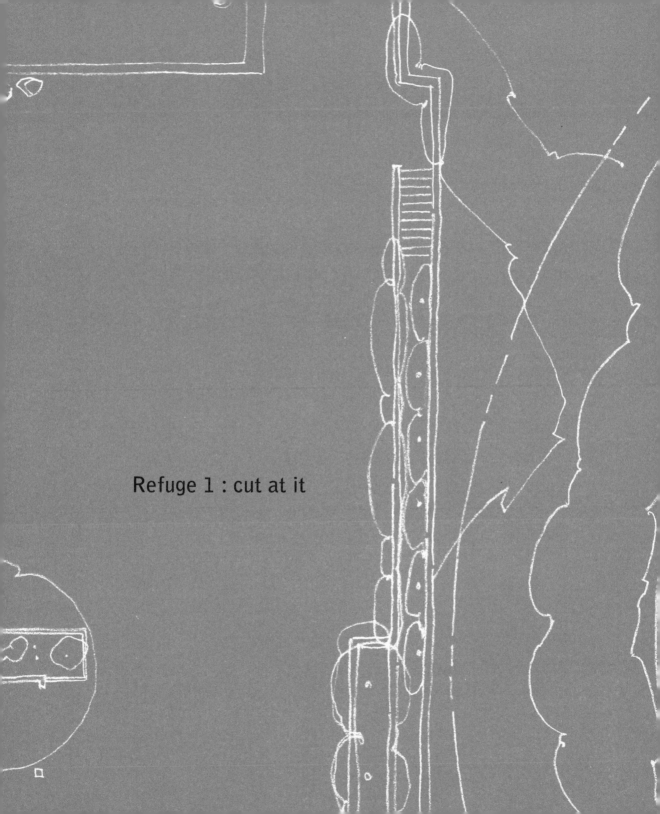

Refuge 1 : cut at it

In a shadowed hard-won enclosure, I take a cut at it, in an intimate moment, lower my eyes.

Motions in a body schema may begin to bunch—as textures in the garden pick up here and here into a congregation listing toward the light—locking with the view.

A daydream of speech becomes a form of movement, eager in the flat pride of riding out and over, even painfully, in the sunshine.

                                The twist begins far

below at my feet. A body pursuing a claim
churns a frenzy of orientation.

Allows a mute part to bruise, swell, bush sideways
on the land shelf, and reset itself into survival under way.

Gardens flicker in and out of existence, can be neglected, the way a woman is saddled by an injury.

A cruel childhood skews the spring fields, I mean future; this day not simply multiplied by the days before it.

To worry whether one can heal or choose the proper height for volume—rejecting manners and miniatures—our attention withstands despair, mobilizes to endure it.

Needing to be written, we move in and out of direction, reaching beyond a lesson to a dappled place where light plays, is happening. The particular entwined with the distributional, there for the taking. To know where we are as a fact—no longer waiting-to-be-seen. Lets itself be felt.

"The persimmon tree is intensely red just this minute!"

"I'm speechless to see myself through your eyes. I almost blush. Does the world dare know all that?"

"You're a good egg. Happy Easter!"

"John and Isabelle invite you to our small outdoor wedding on Sunday, August first, at one o'clock . . . the garden of Carol Valentine, Montecito, California." "You will ride to the wedding site with Isabelle." (Though I had writer's block, I could not fail her, so went early to her house, advised on her corset and shoes.)

Once alone, now alive in the mind of the other, building to achieve her for her. No fences tall or dense, and the achillea weeded diligently.

White flowers on the right, pinks on the left, and the cyclamen diagonaled across the path between.

Dug up what stayed alive and returned it to use.

"Low where I want you to go and feel welcome, and then high to cradle you."

I say right now I want to wear a man's shirt and Paul Smith summer boots—no laces, but a full enclosure. (A vow against tiptoeing and landscape as a profile of thinking.)

Here I am, the architecture close-in, the Valentine entrance, and I will raid it:

"Do I want tall or do I want ——?"

—Greene silences the architect's white wall by planting two eucalyptus trees to whistle over it. The eye hops right up, ears listen branch to moving branch, and the present tense warms what's freshly bare, revealing a woman to herself.

"Space exactly the way I want it."

When the picture holds, my mouth drops again
toward the fetal heart from which it came.

I'm saying as a child I had my habitat.

Climbing a bank and rolling down, up early to write, the repetition of effort, and to know as in any orchard that the uptake is true.

Going as continuity—doing this and that becomes involuntary, like camaraderie, beginnings sprung by an instinct of fullness.

As a tree canopy flutters between a search and my moving language around, its aerial shapes resembling bed hangings.

Later, from inside, awkwardly, trying to be sufficient to it, greet its vast intention perfectly—pollen to pollen, anther and bee—as in placing words into the right season and urging a dented, monocarpic fruit toward harvest.

Too much can blow over into nonexistence. But this a shaggy Shetland journey; spatial design of syntax carries the load, holds the form against danger.

Greene keeps herself low in the airspace. "I back my body as far away from it as I can get and look at it from a long ways away. Then I turn around and look in the opposite direction and see what I can see."

A forty-five-year relationship with the horizontal—volume and line extruded to transparency, gravity given over to a twig chosen for its springiness and reflected in water.

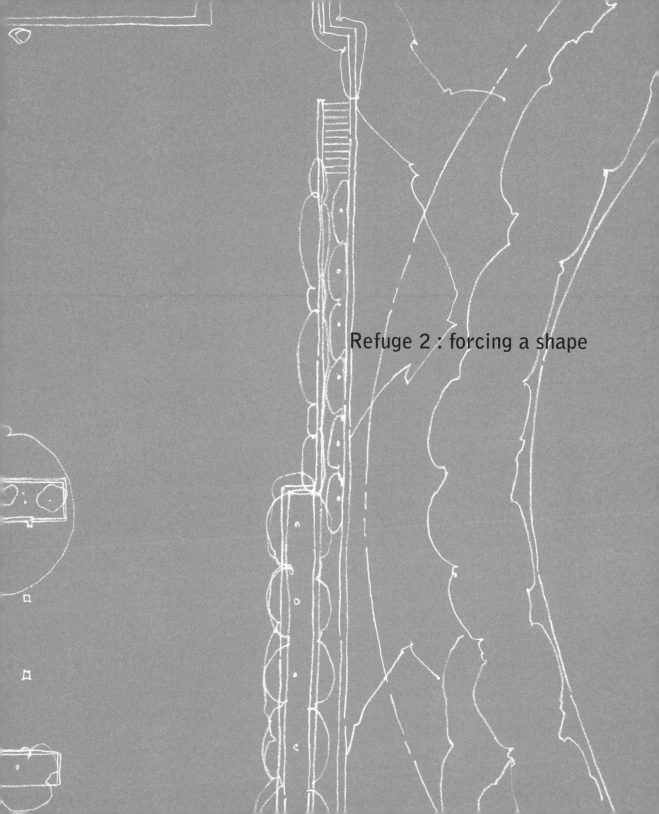

Refuge 2 : forcing a shape

Switching view to scene,

text anchoring description, formalizing as I write, no longer acting it.

Visible from above, ordered, and solid in its insistence. Volume and harmony.

Architect framed it: a panorama, paralysis, expanding from your chest.

Breathe in what you've paid for.

White page a slick of construction talk, prow language,
thrust loose into air,

no surprise naming of vital parts, no reverberation against bone.

Space a gesture. Say, monument.

Redirected creeks/what we thought we wanted: turbulence jostling a linguistic
surface that knows land by appraising it.

Scrape the hillside.

Loud bulldozer erases topsoil, turns,

piles it.

White real estate. Visible inertia. Hot. Isotropic.

Argue over, and back over, hyperbole and level it.

Check—
the excess,
the future,
argue again for view:

All fours still feels strong in the back.
I lumber forward once more to defoliate east or west.
Just as when "Bridge over Troubled Water" was a hit, I wanted very much
a strong kiss.

Move into mouth's house: but don't write myself into

a miniaturized shelter on paper.

Pages can be lost (the image was lost). An aesthetic is a pale egg.

We trust the dictionary allows meaning on more than one side.
See the Englishwoman—did you ask her about the royals yet—fit it in.

Oh, aspect/affect/accent, coughing it into a handkerchief.

On another continent—

dared swing a leg along a French allée, treetops tranquil, a symmetrical club of
green. Progress not neutral; rather what was operable in my legs was the direction
of the landscape architect (the third stabilizing pole, equilibrium of an ideal
number?). When the destination is put in sight, I am a precondition, and the text
a mathematical projection, limited by what I can imagine I can do. Advancing is a
repetition of optimal placement to the horizon. All controlled assurances: at the end
of the lawn, a horse rearing on a plinth and myself in its gaze. Who's to question the
causal geometry between reflex—a proper jerk to the knee—and being carried
away?

—And yet, although not equitable and still in perfect frontal perspective, the motion
feels again alive and mine.

In this enactment of form/format,
beware the charms of journey and horizon as metaphors. They lack embodiment,
the way in my dream a cup flies from my hand and goes confidently, trusted, no
spilling.

I'm saying, scuff too-familiar orientations

: Don't stumble.

A fixed evergreen view permits no anxiety or lottery of collision. At Versailles, the designer, Le Nôtre, took no risks to keep us walking.

European perspective veneered and seeping internationally, over garden walls gilded fountains demonstrate tinkling thinking.

"People ask, 'Where's your focal point?' "

"I hate being told what to look at!"

Perspectival purity a large hand on our knee.

Zigzag path
of abandonment descends out of luck

until this hillside garden flattens the grade, "invites a viewer into the game," an
anamorphosis of creation.

Rehabilitation occurring from immersion, a coherent deformation,
scars in the blue bloom of agave leaves.

At my feet, those agave hunker in white groundcover, and gray slate stones step
through them,

a maturation of matter

proving gain.

"When everything above in the sky is dark—say after a rainstorm at the end of the day—and there's something in the foreground that is brilliantly lit by a low slanting sun, I feel love then. It is just it and me. No separation."

"Bless you, dear one, source of so many good things."
"Would to God we lived closer."

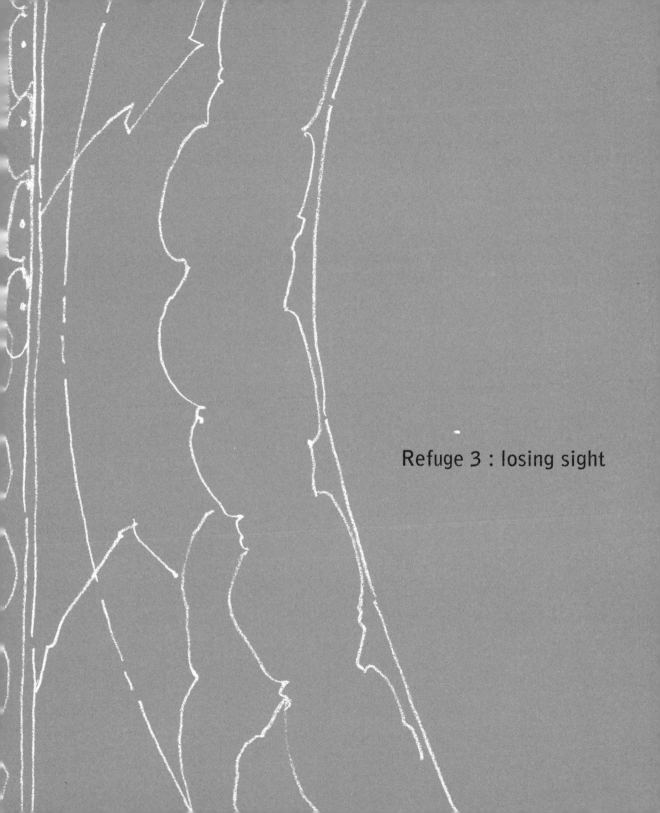

Refuge 3 : losing sight

No more sidling contiguously, as buds break in turn along a limb.
Exhaustion in so much gallant lateralness.
Mulberry stems mahogany with it.

Speak of adverse circumstances. Tight bunch of.

Rub the parts together, the better to remember,
memorially,
as in a valley.

A gloss idles over the garden, aging flowers face one way then another regardless.

The vision was not mine to keep. It slows and fails. "I think we were trying to match ourselves to the idea we had of it."

The garden gone its own way, lost now from the page. Fading effects I could not anticipate.

This wash altogether unseen, jammed in kalanchoe,
needs replanting or call the project done.

Leaning in
one can see what one color, sadness, does to another.

Looking over the wall,
escarpment of acid yellow sedum. Smell it,
and don't know what to do.

"In a nutshell, I've thought about verticals only as line, not as volume."

My own field of groundcovers dense with overoccurrence. Defoliation now the topic.

And yet the land lets me down gently, Greene made it so,
to a white silver field of snow-in-summer.

—the steady heart of the Valentine picture
[across the water toward an urn in the reeds
the most photographed garden scene in the late 20th century, www.]

Greene designed it for her friend, fully each for each, weightless
so no gaze would be shy.

Bare it/bear it, I mean. Absence, in sky's frame.

Wanting to write roughly square and rounded too, for comfort, not talk any more.

Brilliance of neon pink crabapple bloom
shatters around itself. Prospect and drop interchangeable.

Memory of a worn page,
recesses.

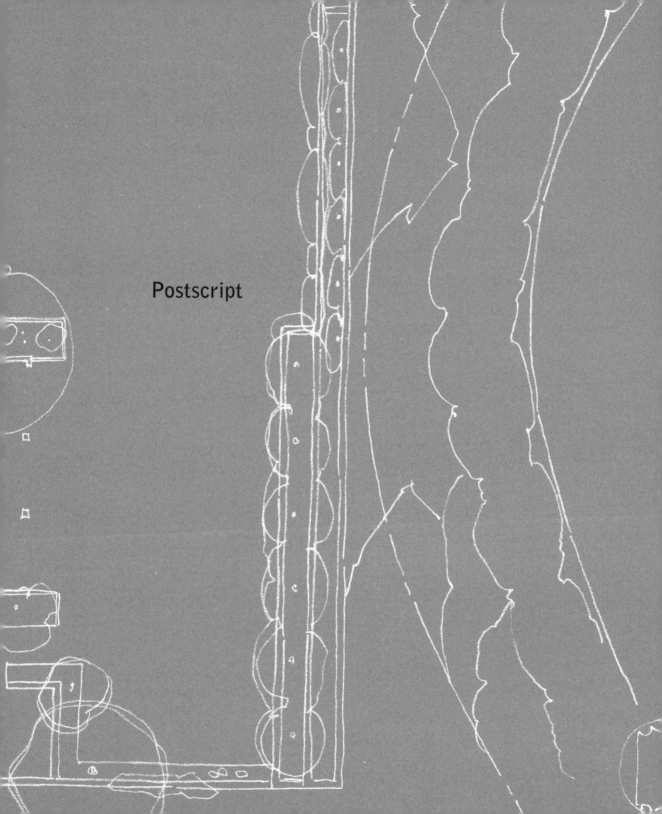

Postscript

At the end of the garden—

an orchard and a field of pork and beans growing in, growing out, no fuss, language earning its keep. Why did I go in to index its presence, risk such a vascular distribution! I tie the why of it into the larger landscape (no upright needed) to make a new out-of-frame direction, transparent churn toward exit, brittle flecks of effort on the insides of my arms, but I keep my chin lifted. The image no longer money but the spring that lost its victorious tones against the trunk of the pomegranate tree and presents itself, if I squat, in a memory beneath my feet.

—Reader, you've come through, across, close by. I'm thinking of you from here, in San Francisco, six miles in from the Pacific Ocean, verifying the lines of my dress, its embroidery, a round-the-back button of my own. Because a garden, like a photograph, can die, I'm placing the flat fact of it here, in the dry, like certainty's stored apples and pears.

ACKNOWLEDGMENTS

Thank you to my poetry friends for reading the manuscript and giving me encouragement or suggesting ways forward: Rusty Morrison, Denise Newman, Susan Gevirtz, Patricia Dienstfrey, and Rena Rosenwasser.

I'm grateful to Headlands Center for the Arts for the community there and a studio overlooking the ocean. Thank you also to Lillian Lovelace for my stay at the tea house.

Special thanks to Nightboat—Stephen Motika, Lindsey Boldt, Andrea Abi-Karam—for their extensive care of this project, and to Margaret Tedesco for the beautiful book design.

Thank you to the editors of the journals in which versions of some of these poems appeared: *New American Writing, Denver Quarterly, Eleven-Eleven, Elderly,* and *Fence.*

I'm grateful to Marion Brenner for the cover photograph; and to Elyse Shafarman, Alexander Technique teacher, for her vivid physical language that I've borrowed on a few pages here.

Isabelle Greene and I have talked for hundreds of hours. Quotes in the manuscript are her words, drawn from those conversations and her notes to me, used here with her permission. Thank you, Isabelle, for everything.

Lastly, mostly, thank you Matt and Jake.

HAZEL WHITE is the author of the poetry collection *Peril as Architectural Enrichment*. She grew up on farms in England and now lives in San Francisco.

NIGHTBOAT BOOKS

Nightboat Books, a nonprofit organization, seeks to develop audiences for
writers whose work resists convention and transcends boundaries. We publish
books rich with poignancy, intelligence, and risk. Please visit our website,
www.nightboat.org, to learn about our titles and how you can support our
future publications.

This book was made possible by a grant from the Topanga Fund, which is
dedicated to promoting the arts and literature of California.

The following individuals have supported the publication of this book. We thank
them for their generosity and commitment to the mission of Nightboat Books:

Elizabeth Motika
Benjamin Taylor

In addition, this book has been made possible, in part, by grants from the
National Endowment for the Arts and the New York State Council on the
Arts Literature Program.